You are to prepare for the
invasion of Europe, for
unless we can go and land
and fight Hitler and beat
his forces on land, we
shall never win this war.
-- Winston Churchill
October 1941

In the last great invasion...

Of the last great war...

The greatest danger for eight men...

...was saving one.

saving private ryan

The Men. The Mission. The Movie.

A Film by Steven Spielberg

Photographs by David James

NEWMARKET PRESS • NEW YORK

Design and compilation copyright © 1998 by Newmarket Press.

Page 17 Text used with permission from *The 101st Airborne at Normandy*
by Mark Bando and published by MBI Publishing, Osceola, Wisconsin.

Pages 15, 19, 21, 22 Text reprinted with the permission of Simon &
Schuster, Inc. from *D-Day: June 6, 1944, The Climactic Battle of World
War II* by Stephen E. Ambrose. New York: Simon & Schuster, 1994.
Copyright © 1994 by Ambrose-Tubbs, Inc. All Rights Reserved.

Pages 28, 33, 36 Text reprinted with the permission of Simon &
Schuster, Inc. from *Citizen Soldiers: The U.S. Army from the Normandy
Beaches to the Bulge to the Surrender of Germany June 7, 1944– May 7,
1945* by Stephen E. Ambrose. New York: Simon & Schuster, 1997.
Copyright © 1997 by Ambrose-Tubbs Inc. All Rights Reserved.

Pages 24-5, 29, 31 *Voices of D-Day: The Story of the Allied Invasion
Told by Those Who Were There*. Edited by Ronald J. Drez. Baton Rouge:
Louisiana State University Press, 1994. Copyright © 1994 by The
Eisenhower Center for Leadership Studies. All Rights Reserved.

10 9 8 7 6 5 4 3 2

ISBN: 1-55704-370-1 (hc); 1-55704-371-X (pb)

Library of Congress Cataloging-in-Publication Data
is available upon request.

 Published by Newmarket Press • New York

This book is published simultaneously in
the United States and in Canada.

Quantity Purchases
Companies, professional groups, clubs, and other organizations may
qualify for special terms when ordering quantities of this title. For
information, write Special Sales, Newmarket Press, 18 East 48th Street,
New York, NY 10017, call (212) 832-3575, or fax (212) 832-3629.

Edited by Linda Sunshine.

Design by Timothy Shaner, Night & Day Design.

DreamWorks Project Executive: Jerry Schmitz
DreamWorks Photo Editor: Boyd Peterson
DreamWorks Art Director: Randy Nellis

Produced by Newmarket Productions, a division of Newmarket
Publishing and Communications Company: Esther Margolis, director;
Keith Hollaman, editor; Frank DeMaio, production manager.

Manufactured in the United States of America
First Edition

INTRODUCTION

Set during and immediately following the invasion of Normandy, *Saving Private Ryan* tells the story of a squad of American soldiers on a dangerous mission to find Private James Ryan whose three brothers have been killed in combat. On direct orders from Washington, Captain John Miller leads his men deep behind enemy lines. As the squad pushes on, the men find themselves asking: Why is one man worth risking the lives of eight?

Amid the chaos and terror of those days in early June 1944, this remarkable story searches to find decency in the sheer madness of war.

While preparing to film *Saving Private Ryan*, hundreds of people spent countless hours researching and re-creating the battles, the landscape, and the destruction of France during those days. One thousand soldiers were employed in filming the landing on Omaha Beach. Original landing boats, guns, and gear were restored to working order. While shooting the battle scenes in strict chronological order, tens of thousands of rounds of ammunition were fired. Every effort was made to capture the harsh reality of war as authentically as possible.

World War II was perhaps the pivotal event of the twentieth century and a defining moment for America and the world. It shifted the borders of the globe, forever changed those who survived it, and shaped the past five decades.

D - D A Y

The U.S. Army's infantry divisions were not elite, by definition, but they had some outstanding characteristics.

The American Selective Service System was just that, selective. One-third of the men called to service were rejected after physical examinations, making the average draftee brighter, healthier, and better educated than the average American. He was twenty-six years old, five feet eight inches tall, weighed 144 pounds, had a thirty-three-and-a-half-inch chest, and a thirty-one-inch waist. After thirteen weeks of basic training, he'd gained seven pounds (and converted many of his original pounds from fat to muscle) and added at least an inch to his chest. Nearly half the draftees were high-school graduates; one in ten had some college. As Geoffrey Perret puts it in his history of the U.S. Army in World War II, "These were the best-educated enlisted men of any army in history."

At the end of 1943 the U.S. Army was the greenest army in the world. Of the nearly fifty infantry, armored, and airborne divisions selected for participation in the campaign in northwest Europe, only two—the 1st Infantry and the 82nd Airborne—had been in combat.

This posed problems and caused apprehension, but it had a certain advantage. According to Pvt. Carl Weast of the U.S. 5th Ranger Battalion, "A veteran infantryman is a terrified infantryman." Sgt. Carwood Lipton of the 506th Parachute Infantry Regiment (PIR) of the 101st Airborne commented, "I took chances on D-Day I would never have taken later in the war. . . ."

For a direct frontal assault on a prepared enemy position, men who have not seen what a bullet or a land mine or an exploding mortar round can do to a human body are preferable to men who have seen the carnage. Men in their late teens or early twenties have a feeling of invulnerability, as seen in the remark of Charles East of the 29th Division. Told by his commanding officer on the eve of D-Day that nine out of ten would become casualties in the ensuing campaign, East looked at the man to his left, then at the man to his right, and thought to himself, "You poor bastards."

—An Excerpt from *D-Day: June 6, 1944*
The Climactic Battle of World War II
by Stephen E. Ambrose

The Men.

June 6, 1944

OFFICE OF THE REGIMENTAL COMMANDER

Soldiers of the Regiment: D-Day

Today, and as you read this, you
are en route to that great adventure
for which you have trained for over
two years.

Tonight is the night of nights.

Tomorrow throughout the whole of our
homeland and the Allied world the
bells will ring out the tidings that
you have arrived, and the invasion
for liberation has begun.

The hopes and prayers of your dear
ones accompany you, the confidence
of your high commanders goes with
you. The fears of the Germans are
about to become a reality.

Let us strike hard. When the going is
tough, let us go harder. Imbued with
faith in the rightness of our cause,
and the power of our might, let us
annihilate the enemy where found.

May God be with each of you fine
soldiers. By your actions let us
justify His faith in us.

Colonel Robert Sink
(Memo to his 506th Troopers)

People of Western Europe: A landing was made this morning on the coast of France by troops of the Allied Expeditionary Force...

...I call upon all who love freedom to stand with us now. Together we shall achieve victory.
-- Dwight D. Eisenhower
Broadcast on D-Day

Lt. Den Brotheridge fired a full clip of thirty-two rounds from his Sten gun. Those were the first shots fired by the 175,000 British, American, Canadian, Free French, Polish, Norwegian, and other nationalities in the Allied Expeditionary Force set to invade Normandy in the next twenty-four hours.
— Stephen E. Ambrose, D-Day

So the GI hitting the beach in the first wave at Omaha would have to get through the minefields in the Channel without his LST blowing up, then get from ship to shore in a Higgins boat taking fire from inland batteries, then work his way through an obstacle-studded tidal flat of some 150 meters crisscrossed by machine gun and rifle fire, with big shells whistling by and mortars exploding all around, to find his first protection behind the shingle. There he would be caught in a triple crossfire--machine guns and heavy artillery from the sides, small arms from the front, mortars coming down from above.

-- Stephen E. Ambrose, D-Day

About seven or eight in the morning, we were being urged by braver and more sensible noncoms and one or two surviving officers to get off the beach and up the bluffs to higher ground. More men from other landing craft behind us were making it across the beach and joining the congestion at the seawall. It would be some time before enough courage returned for us to attempt movement up the slopes and up the beach. Scared, worried, and often praying, I had been busy helping some of the wounded; most of the time, moving in

a crouched position, a few of us helped move the helpless to
secure areas. Once or twice I was able to control my fear enough
to race across the sand to drag a helpless GI from drowning in the
incoming tide. That was the extent of my bravery that morning. Then
clear thinking replaced some of our fear, and many of us accepted
the fact that we had to get off the beach or die where we were.
We got off the beach.

    -- Harry Parley, Private First Class, Company E, from Voices of D-Day

Normandy was a soldier's battle. It belonged to the riflemen, machine gunners, mortarmen, tankers, and artillery men who were on the front lines. There was no room for maneuver. There was no opportunity for subtlety. There was a simplicity to the fighting: for the Germans, to hold; for the Americans, to attack.

-- Stephen E. Ambrose, _Citizen Soldiers_

As ranking noncom, I tried to get my men off the boat and make it somehow to the cliff, but it was horrible--men frozen in the sand, unable to move. My radio man had his head blown off three yards from me. The beach was covered with bodies--men with no legs, no arms--God, it was awful. It was absolutely terrible.
-- Harry Bare, Sergeant, Company F, 1st Squadron, from Voices of D-Day

There was thousands of ships, and we could see landing
boats of American troops. Then came thousands of men at
one time coming on land and running over the beach.
This is the first time I shoot on living men, and
I go to the machine gun and I shoot, I shoot,
I shoot! For each American I see fall,
there came ten hundred other ones!
-- Franz Rachmann, Private,
German 352nd Division,
from Voices of D-Day

But the hardest lesson to teach in training, the most difficult rule to follow in combat, is to keep moving when fired on. Every instinct makes a soldier want to hug the ground.
                    -- Stephen E. Ambrose, _Citizen Soldiers_

By June 30, the Americans had brought 71,000 vehicles over the beaches (of a planned 110,000) and 452,000 soldiers (of a planned 579,000)...It had eleven divisions in the battle, as scheduled, plus the 82nd and the 101st Airborne... The Americans had evacuated 27,000 casualties. About 11,000 GIs had been killed in action or died of their wounds, 1,000 were missing in action, and 3,400 wounded men had been returned to duty. So the total active duty strength of U.S. First Army in Normandy on June 30 was 413,000. German strength on the American front was somewhat less, while German losses against the combined British-Canadian-American forces were 47,500.

-- Stephen E. Ambrose, Citizen Soldiers

The Mission.

29 ON MILLER

Miller and the others look around,
stunned -- we did it. We're alive. After
the beach, it's more than any of them
expected. Nobody says anything, because
there really aren't words to express the
moment. We're here. It's a fact.

Sarge reaches down, picks up a handful of
sand, and pours it into a container that is
already premarked "France." He screws
the tin lid back on and puts it back in his
pack next to two similar tin cans upon
which are crudely inscribed in smeared
blue ink "Africa" and "Italy."

--from the screenplay

Corporal Upham

Sergeant Horvath

Private Jackson

Private Mellish

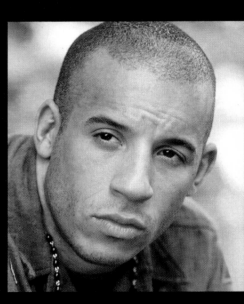

Private Caparzo

ON MILLER AND REIBEN

REIBEN
This goes against every-
thing the army taught me.
Makes no sense—

MILLER
What doesn't make sense,
Reiben?

REIBEN
The math, sir. Of this
mission. Maybe you could
explain it to me.

MILLER
What do you want to
know?

REIBEN
Well, sir, in purely
arithmetic terms, what's
the sense in risking eight
guys to save one?

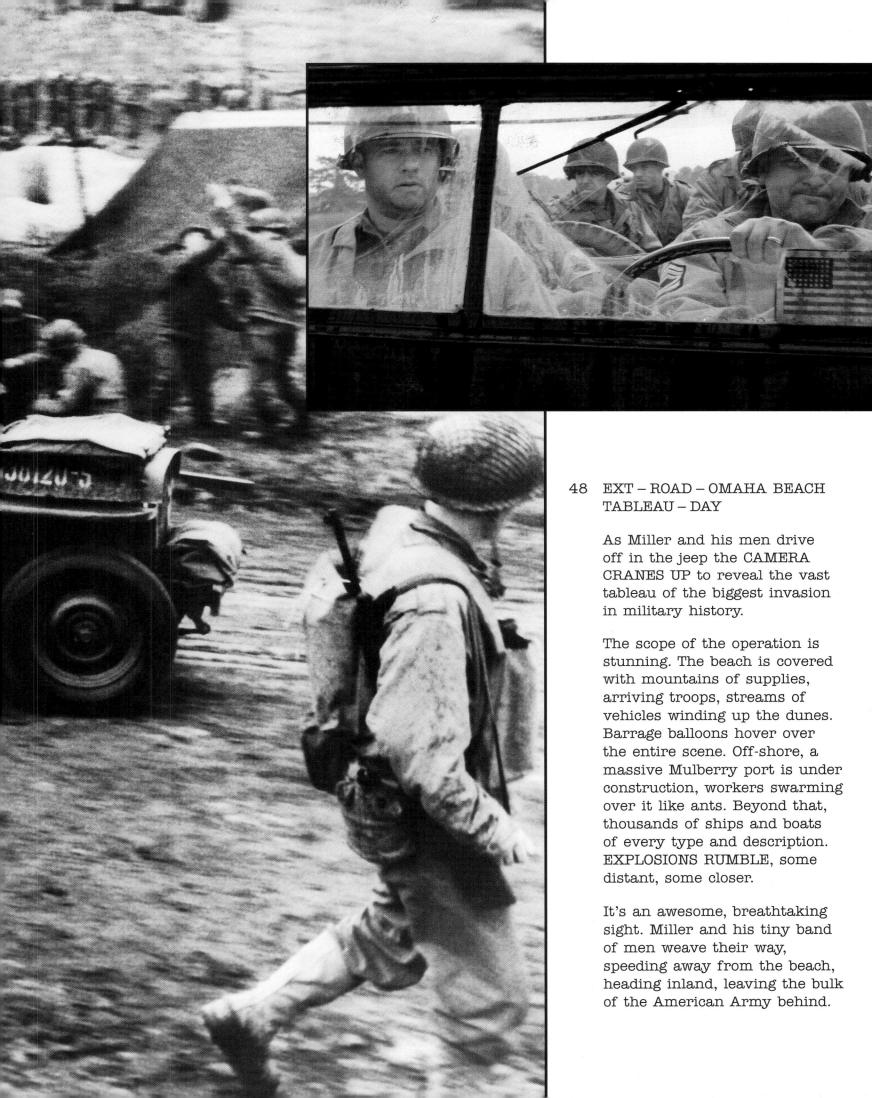

48   EXT – ROAD – OMAHA BEACH
      TABLEAU – DAY

As Miller and his men drive
off in the jeep the CAMERA
CRANES UP to reveal the vast
tableau of the biggest invasion
in military history.

The scope of the operation is
stunning. The beach is covered
with mountains of supplies,
arriving troops, streams of
vehicles winding up the dunes.
Barrage balloons hover over
the entire scene. Off-shore, a
massive Mulberry port is under
construction, workers swarming
over it like ants. Beyond that,
thousands of ships and boats
of every type and description.
EXPLOSIONS RUMBLE, some
distant, some closer.

It's an awesome, breathtaking
sight. Miller and his tiny band
of men weave their way,
speeding away from the beach,
heading inland, leaving the bulk
of the American Army behind.

54   EXT. HEDGEROW CART ROAD – DAY

Miller walks point. His men follow warily. It's hot. They're
exhausted. Upham looks miserable, weighed down like a pack
horse with all the B.A.R. ammunition, slapping at horseflies.
They talk quietly, their eyes scanning.

UPHAM
"War educates the senses, calls into action the will, perfects the physical constitution, brings men into such swift and close collision in critical moments that man measures man."

MILLER
I guess that's Emerson's way to look on the bright side.

CAPARZO
Captain. Decent thing to do would be to at least take the kids
down the road to the next town.

MILLER
We're not here to do the decent thing, Caparzo. We're here to
follow orders.

Miller watches his men go. He gives himself a second and looks at what remains of the once lovely village, now nothing more than rubble. Hamill steps up next to him. Though strangers, Miller and Hamill speak like tired old friends.

                    HAMILL (CONT'D)
          What do you hear? How's it all
          falling together?

                    MILLER
          Beachhead's secure but it's slow
          goin'. Monty's takin' his time
          getting to Caen, we can't move
          'til he's ready.

                    HAMILL
          That guy's over-rated.

                    MILLER
          No kiddin'.

Hamill shakes his head and sighs.

                    HAMILL
          We gotta take Caen to take St. Lo.

                    MILLER
          And we gotta take St. Lo to take
          Valognes.

                    HAMILL
          Gotta take Valognes to take
          Cherbourg.

                    MILLER
          Gotta take Cherbourg to take
          Paris.

                    HAMILL
          Gotta take Paris to take Berlin.

                    MILLER
          Gotta take Berlin to take a boat
          home.

MILLER

Every time you kill one of your men, you
tell yourself you just saved the lives of
two, three, ten, a hundred others. You
know how many men I've lost under
my command?

SARGE

How many?

MILLER
(instantly)

Ninety-four. So that must mean I've
saved the lives of ten times that number.
Maybe twenty, right? See it's simple.
It lets you always choose the mission
over men.

SARGE

Except this time the mission is a man.

Miller looks at Sarge now. His eyes hard.

MILLER

And Ryan better be worth it. He better
go home and cure some disease or invent
a new longer-lasting lightbulb.

MILLER
Tell me, Reiben, you had to do it again, how'd you think you'd react the next time?

REIBEN
Me? I'd shoot myself 'fore I ever got off the damn boat.

Ryan stands, indicates the other guys in his unit.

RYAN (CONT'D)
Hell, these guys deserve to go home as much as I do. They've fought just as hard.

MILLER
Is that what I'm supposed to tell your mother, she gets another flag?

RYAN
You can tell her that when you found me, I was with the only brothers I had left. And that there was no way I was deserting them. I think she'd understand that.

He and Miller stare at each other.

SARGE

I don't know. Part of me thinks the kid's right, he asks what he's done to deserve this. He wants to stay here, fine. Let's leave him and go home. But then another part of me thinks what if by some miracle we stay then actually make it out of here. Someday we might look back on this and decide that saving Private Ryan was the one decent thing we were able to pull out of this whole godawful mess. Like you said, Capt'n, maybe we do that, we <u>all</u> earn the right to go home.

118 ANGLE ON STREET

—and thunderous hell breaks loose as the HAWKINS MINES
DETONATE massively along both sides of the street. The walls
blow out towards the infantry, taking them down with
concussion and shrapnel, killing at least a dozen men...

The MACHINE GUNS OPEN FIRE at the same moment, turning
the street into a killing zone

156 THE LAST SANDBAG EMPLACEMENT

... and then the Tiger FIRES ITS CANNON. THE EXPLOSION TEARS THE WORLD APART, spinning it upside-down, ripping the air with heat and shrapnel...

... and everything goes quiet, as if the sound has drained out of the world. We're left with sounds that are remote, faint, surreal, disembodied...

158   RESUME NORMAL SPEED AND SOUND:

...<u>as a P-51 MUSTANG swoops grandly over the bridge.</u> Tank-buster. It peels overhead, no longer with the sound of voices but with a THROATY ROAR OF A PACKARD ENGINE.

The Movie.

Although I admire war movies and have seen many of them, I wasn't really looking to make a World War II film. I didn't want to shoot the picture as a Hollywood gung-ho Rambo kind of extravaganza. I wanted the audience to be fairly uneasy sitting through the invasion of Normandy.

Our approach to the movie was the way a documentary filmmaker would have approached it in, for example, John Ford's unit shooting the South Pacific War or George Stevens's unit shooting the European campaign. We just had a camera. Janusz stripped all the glossy filters and the filaments from the lenses so they were just like the kind of lenses they actually used in the Second World War. We shot a lot of the war sequences with the shutter speed used by those Bell and Howell cameras of the 1940s for making newsreels.

The audience won't feel much difference except, if we've done our jobs, they will think we were actually on the beach on D-Day.

    —Steven Spielberg

"In boot camp, Captain Dye said to us,
'I want you to bring honor to the fraternity
of men who died for your freedom.'"
-- Barry Pepper, actor

The actors in boot camp.
(Left to right) Front row: Barry Pepper, Tom Hanks, Tom Sizemore, Ed Burns, Capt. Dale Dye, Vin Diesel, Adam Goldberg, Giovanni Ribisi, Jeremy Davies. Back row: Assistants to Dale Dye.

We went through an extensive training period in the woods for the better part of a week, which helped us understand about the gear and what it's like to slog this stuff around. We're essentially playing guys who are tired and miserable and want to go home. Great physical demands are being made of them constantly.

We hiked all over the place; it was rainy and cold and wet. We slept on the ground and ate food that came out of cans, heated up over little tiny stoves. Dale was constantly yelling at us because we were doing things wrong. We learned various combat techniques but that wasn't as important as the experience itself.

We were up at five in the morning, carrying very heavy stuff on our backs all day long, and we only had a few moments to lie down in the grass and maybe go to sleep. But then we had to get up again; the day's not over until two in the morning.

Now we do that in microcosm as actors, but all of us will tell you that we couldn't have played our parts without experiencing what Dale Dye put us through.

—Tom Hanks

I'm not a wilderness guy. I mean, I'm like the guy in *On the Waterfront* who says, "The crickets make me nervous." I'm a very New York guy. And so already, sleeping out in the wilderness is a stretch for me. And then to sleep under harsh rain conditions and be woken up after only a few hours following a really hard day—it was very rough.

But it did serve two functions. One was the brotherhood. There could not have been a more bonding experience. The other is that our relationship with Tom Hanks couldn't have been set up any better. Every single guy in the platoon wanted to leave early except for Tom who was the only one who said we should stay an extra few days. And it was so appropriate because he's playing the Captain who has the most endurance.

— Vin Diesel, actor

I didn't want to go to boot camp. I'm an actor, I'm going to *act* like a marine, why do I have to *be* a marine? It's called acting, not "being."

We were taken to this forest and given a blanket, no pillow. It was hard to sleep on the ground! In L.A., I don't sleep on the ground, I sleep in a bed.

We got up at four in the morning and ran five miles and did all these push-ups and sit-ups. You don't eat anything and your feet stick out of the tent at night! And since I'm the Sarge, I have to walk around and kick the guys in the feet to wake them up in the morning.

This is nuts, but we really went through something like the men in the movie experienced. In the field, the men would go to their sergeant to voice their grievances and then the sarge went to the captain and that's how it happened in our boot camp. The other actors, Eddie Burns, Vin Diesel, Adam Goldberg, and Jeremy Davies, would come to me to say, "I can't do this."

But then something happened to all of us. We really learned that no one does anything alone in a war. It's all about teamwork—if the other guy's sick or can't get his gear on, you stop and help him out. That's what the marines are all about—it's a brotherhood. We got just a taste of that and it brought us closer together so that when we started shooting we felt a bond.

Still, after boot camp, the first thing I did was drink a Diet Coke.

—Tom Sizemore, actor

Top: **Boot camp.**
Left: (Left to right) Tom Hanks, Capt. Dale Dye, Vin Diesel, Tom Sizemore.

"Captain Dye only referred to us by our character names. It was sort of like Stanislavsky running boot camp."
--Adam Goldberg, actor

We spent a week together living out in the woods in tents. It was the worst experience of my life. It really was. It was physically exhausting and tough; it was really hard on all of us. But we got a real sense of what these guys went through.

We spent a lot of time talking with Captain Dye, who'd been in Vietnam and Desert Storm. Every night we'd ask him questions about his experiences. What was your relationship with the guys you're serving with? What was it like to lose a friend? And how terrifying was it when you were behind enemy lines and walking around at night in the woods without being able to see five feet in front of you? What's going on in your head?

—Ed Burns, actor

"Steven says, 'Real is the watchword,' and if it looks horrible on screen, well, so it is in combat. The more horrible we can show it, the more people will understand the nobility of the sacrifice that those men made."
--Capt. Dale Dye, USMC (ret.)

The Battle on Omaha Beach scene. (Left to right) Tom Sanders, Production Designer; Steven Spielberg, Director; Tom Hanks, Actor; Capt. Dale Dye, Senior Military Advisor.

I believe there is a certain core spirit within an American fighting man, within a fighting man of any nationality. A certain heart and spirit is common with all fighting men. Actors—who are like dry sponges until you pour on the water—need to be immersed in the rigorous lifestyle, in the horrors facing infantrymen and combat people all over the world. So to the extent that insurance and lifestyles will allow, I immerse those actors in that lifestyle. I take them to the field, I make them eat rations, I shoot at them with blank ammunition, I beat them up, I beat on them, I make them crawl and sleep in the mud and the cold and the dirt. And when they come out the other end, if I've done my job successfully, they have an inkling of what it's like—the deprivations, the hardships people endure to serve their country in the military.

—Capt. Dale Dye, USMC (ret.)

For locations, I looked all around France, Ireland, and England. Ireland had an area that looked exactly like Normandy. The landscape and the beaches were so similar it was uncanny.

We had to have beach access, so we were also looking for a place with a harbor. We needed a particular kind of tide to have a certain amount of beach left when the tide was in, for the crew on the beach.

Also, we needed a location where we could house a thousand-man army and a 45-man crew.

Having worked in Ireland before, we knew we could hire its army, which was a key element. Without a trained army to jump out of the boats and storm the beach with experience, we'd have to train a lot of extras. We needed regiments. We had to get them ready every day and have them on the set.

Logistically, it was a nightmare.

—Tom Sanders, production designer

Crew members on the beach in Ireland.
(Left to right) Steve Painter, Make-up Effects Artist; Mitch Dubin, Camera Operator; Maxie McDonald, Prop Master; Jim Kwiatkowski, Key Grip; Neil Corbould, Special Effects; Janusz Kaminski, Director of Photography; Steven Spielberg, Director; Ian Bryce, Producer; Sergio Mimica, First Assistant Director; Chris Haarhoff, Steadi-Cam/ Camera Operator; Lisa Dean Kavanaugh, Set Decorator.

The tanks and other vehicles were fairly easy to find but not the landing craft. We found some in England and a couple in Scotland, but, interestingly enough, the majority of them were in Palm Springs, California.

We bought them and built cradles to ship them over. They arrived in Southampton and we sent them to a refurbishing yard. Then we put them on another ship and sent them to Ireland. It was a pretty big moving operation for the transportation department.

There are twelve of these landing craft in the movie and several hundred in the background.

—Ian Bryce, producer

One day we were out there on the boats and the Irish sea was really rough. It was a cold, stormy day and the Higgins boats were slamming pretty hard, bouncing and pounding through the surf; the chop was like four to five feet swells. A few of the guys around me were getting sick. We were getting really upset, as in reality, not our characters. We were just very nervous about the water and being in the boats and we got this incredible feeling of impending doom.

It gave me this minute sensation of what it must've been like out there. It was really scary for me. My mind just started to wander and think about how afraid these young guys must have been. And they were so tired and soaking wet. They had all their layers of wool clothing and all their gear and ammunition and when they stepped off the boat, they saw all their pals dying around them. They were so exhausted and seasick and all they could do was crawl up those beaches. And thousands of them lay dead in no time at all. It's unthinkable.

—Barry Pepper, actor

It took us three months to gather the 2,000 weapons that we used in the film. About 500 of them were capable of firing blanks, the others were rubber. They all needed dusting, cleaning, and painting each evening.

We brought them all from England. Some of our weapons came from Germany, but a lot of the American artillery is in England.

Of course, we had to deactivate certain weapons and make sure they weren't capable of firing live ammunition.

—Simon Atherton, armourer

First, I respond emotionally to what the film should look like; the words go through my heart and then I try to put them on the screen.

There were many parallels between this movie and *Schindler's List*. Both were World War II dramas that I envisioned in a semi-documentary style, using hand-held cameras for images that were full of texture. My other idea was to subtract some of the color from the film in a desaturation process done after the movie is shot. About

sixty percent of the color was extracted from the final negative.

I didn't want blue skies, I didn't want any clouds. Through the whole course of the movie, there's virtually not a single shot of blue sky. I was going for this kind of burned-out, bleary sky, and I used various techniques to achieve these visuals. For example, Panavision in Los Angeles prepared a particular set of lenses for me. They extracted the protective coating inside the lens so the images were slightly more defused and prone to flares, and the skies were burned out. The whole image was softer without being out of focus.

Another technique was that we used a different shadow degree to achieve a certain staccato in the actors' movement. We got a crispness of explosions. Everything we shot became slightly, just slightly, more realistic.

—Janusz Kaminski, cinematographer

We're at Hatfield Aerodrome, which is north of London. When we started here, this was a grass field. We decided that it would be better to build a river for environmental reasons and for control. We started from scratch, dug the river back here, and put in the bridge.

We had to build these buildings because we couldn't find anything like this in Europe. It's all historically accurate.

After three trips to France, we built a model of a French village. We made this whole town in model form and then we slowly carved out the places where the bombs would've hit.

The model for this whole town took us five weeks to build in Los Angeles and then we shipped it over here. It's a great tool for the director and the cinematographer to use. They see the set-up in color and in three dimensions.

—Tom Sanders, production designer

Following page: **Aerial view of the set at Hatfield Aerodrome, which was formerly a grass field.**

Many years ago I was working as a bellman in a hotel, and the guy who picked up the dry cleaning every afternoon and brought it back in the morning was a D-Day veteran. He was away on vacation for two weeks, and when he returned I asked him how it went. He said, "Well, it was both good and it was bad."

He told me that he was a veteran of the 101st Airborne, the paratroopers who jumped on June 5th. Every year he went to this reunion. But every year there were fewer and fewer guys among the group of survivors.

As soon as I read the script for *Saving Private Ryan*, he was one of the first guys who came to my mind.

As a film subject, World War II, by and large, is a never-ending, fascinating lesson for an actor. There was so much about the invasion of Europe that translates in actor's terms: motivations and movement, even the props and costumes.

We started this movie with the utter chaos and shambles of Omaha Beach, which really put everything in its proper perspective. We had lines we never even shot. It was a waste of time to try and establish any kind of rapport amongst us after all the carnage we witnessed.

If we hadn't started with D-Day, and I think Steven would probably agree, we would've wasted an awful lot of time trying to establish other stuff that wasn't important. After D-Day the whole point was: Let's find this guy and get home.

There are a lot of brilliant World War II movies, but it's been thirty years since a real chronicle epic of the war has been made.

For our generation who grew up on various World War II movies, I think that war has a kind of mythical memory connected to being kids and having fathers who were in the war as well as the influence of all those television shows and movies. For the younger generation, it's ancient history. They probably think Normandy is a country right next to Sweden.

Still, we don't want to lecture an audience. We are trying to communicate to them that mere mortals, people who are the same age as themselves, had to be called upon to make this hard sacrifice in service to mankind. From a purely humanistic point of view, I think it's important to go back and examine this piece of history.

—Tom Hanks, actor

Any scene involving the characters as they explore their fragilities are the ones that surprise me the most. I knew that the invasion scenes would work because Steven Spielberg is so accurate about the military and technical aspects. The D-Day landing is very startling, very dramatic, but it's not surprising. But when the actors and the director bring the smaller moments to life, that's when I get startled and I say, "Hey, I didn't write that. Great!"
— Robert Rodat, screenwriter

As a young director observing Spielberg's approach to directing, I've noticed that he's like an undefeated boxer who is so good that he could approach the game without having to plan his shots or his strategy. He can come in, look at the situation, and pick out his shots immediately. He knows how they'll connect and how they'll cut together, so he cuts as he goes along. It's amazing. I've never seen anyone work that fast. Also, he's confident enough with himself to put the priority on the work. If an actor, or anybody else involved in the production, has an idea or a concept, he's completely receptive, which makes all the actors real comfortable.

—Vin Diesel, actor

Left: (Left to right) Tom Hanks, Steven Spielberg, Ed Burns.
Top: Steven Spielberg, Matt Damon
Right: Jeremy Davies

"The real stars on the beach were the members of the Irish army who helped us re-create the largest manned invasion in history."
-- Steven Spielberg

Right: **Members of the Irish army in full regalia on the first day of filming on the beach in Ireland.**

"Omaha Beach was a nightmare. Even now
it brings pain to recall what happened
there on June 6, 1944. I have returned
many times to honor the valiant men
who died on that beach. They should
never be forgotten. Nor should those
who lived to carry the day by the
slimmest of margins. Every man who
set foot on Omaha Beach that
day was a hero."
--General Omar Bradley, 1974

DREAMWORKS PICTURES *and* PARAMOUNT PICTURES
present

An AMBLIN ENTERTAINMENT *Production*

In association with MUTUAL FILM COMPANY

saving private ryan

Directed by STEVEN SPIELBERG

Written by ROBERT RODAT

Produced by STEVEN SPIELBERG & IAN BRYCE

Produced by MARK GORDON & GARY LEVINSOHN

Director of Photography JANUSZ KAMINSKI, A.S.C.

Production Designer TOM SANDERS

Film Editor MICHAEL KAHN, A.C.E.

Music by JOHN WILLIAMS

Costume Designer JOANNA JOHNSTON

Co-Producers BONNIE CURTIS
& ALLISON LYON SEGAN

Casting by DENISE CHAMIAN, C.S.A.

Captain Miller
TOM HANKS

Sergeant Horvath
TOM SIZEMORE

Private Reiben
EDWARD BURNS

Private Jackson
BARRY PEPPER

Private Mellish
ADAM GOLDBERG

Private Caparzo
VIN DIESEL

T/4 Medic Wade
GIOVANNI RIBISI

Corporal Upham
JEREMY DAVIES

Private Ryan
MATT DAMON

Associate Producer/ Production Manager	MARK HUFFAM
First Assistant Director	SERGIO MIMICA-GEZZAN
Second Assistant Director	ADAM GOODMAN
Associate Producer	KEVIN DE LA NOY
Sound Designer	GARY RYDSTROM
Special Effects Supervisor	NEIL CORBOULD
Special Effects Floor Supervisor	CLIVE BEARD
Stunt Coordinator	SIMON CRANE
Supervising Art Director	DANIEL T. DORRANCE
Set Decorator	LISA DEAN KAVANAUGH
Senior Military Advisor	CAPT. DALE DYE, USMC (ret)
U.K. Casting by	PRISCILLA JOHN

THE CAST

Captain Miller	TOM HANKS
Sergeant Horvath	TOM SIZEMORE
Private Reiben	EDWARD BURNS
Private Jackson	BARRY PEPPER
Private Mellish	ADAM GOLDBERG
Private Caparzo	VIN DIESEL
T/4 Medic Wade	GIOVANNI RIBISI
Corporal Upham	JEREMY DAVIES
Private Ryan	MATT DAMON
Captain Hamill	TED DANSON
Sergeant Hill	PAUL GIAMATTI
Lieutenant Colonel Anderson	DENNIS FARINA
Steamboat Willie	JOERG STADLER
Corporal Henderson	MAXIMILIAN MARTINI
Toynbe	DYLAN BRUNO
Weller	DANIEL CERQUEIRA
Parker	DEMETRI GORITSAS
Trask	IAN PORTER
Rice	GARY SEFTON
Garrity	JULIAN SPENCER
Wilson	STEVE GRIFFIN
Lyle	WILLIAM MARSH
Fallon	MARC CASS
Major Hoess	MARKUS NAPIER
Ramelle Paratroopers	NEIL FINNIGHAN
	PETER MILES
Field HQ Major	PAUL GARCIA
Field HQ Aide	SEAMUS McQUADE
Coxswain	RONALD LONGRIDGE
Delancey	ADAM SHAW
Lieutenant Briggs	ROLF SAXON
Radioman	COREY JOHNSON

Soldiers on the Beach

LOCLANN AIKEN	JOHN BARNETT
MacLEAN BURKE	VICTOR BURKE
AIDEN CONDRON	PASCHAL FRIEL
SHANE HAGAN	PAUL HICKEY
SHANE JOHNSON	LAIRD MacINTOSH
BRIAN MAYNARD	MARTIN McDOUGALL
MARK PHILLIPS	LEE ROSEN
ANDREW SCOTT	MATTHEW SHARP
VINCENT WALSH	GRAHAME WOOD

Corporal	JOHN SHARIAN
Boyle	GLENN WRAGE
Senior Medical Officer	CROFTON HARDESTER
Czech Wermacht Soldier	MARTIN HUB
Goldman	RAPH TAYLOR
Private Boyd	NIGEL WHITMEY
Private Hastings	SAM ELLIS
German #1	ERICH REDMAN
German #2	TILO KEINER
German #3/ Voice on Bullhorn	STEPHAN GROTHGAR
Jean	STEPHAN CORNICARD
Jean's Wife	MICHELLE EVANS
Jean's Son	MARTIN BEATON
Jean's Daughter	ANNA MAGUIRE
Minnesota Ryan	NATHAN FILLION
Lieutenant DeWindt	LELAND ORSER

Paratrooper Lieutenant	MICHAEL MANTAS
Paratrooper Oliver	DAVID VEGH
Paratrooper Michaelson	RYAN HURST
Paratrooper Joe	NICK BROOKS
Paratrooper #1	SAM SCUDDER
Old French Man	JOHN WALTERS
Old French Woman	DOROTHY GRUMBAR
MP Lieutenant	JAMES INNES-SMITH
General Marshall	HARVE PRESNELL
War Department Colonels	DALE DYE
	BRYAN CRANSTON
War Department Captain	DAVID WOHL
War Department Lieutenant	ERIC LOREN
War Department Clerk	VALERIE COLGAN
Mrs. Margaret Ryan	AMANDA BOXER
Ryan as Old Man	HARRISON YOUNG
Old Mrs. Ryan	KATHLEEN BYRON
Ryan's Son	ROB FREEMAN
Ryan's Grandson	THOMAS GIZBERT

Stunts

ANDY BENNETT	JINDRICH KLAUS
PAVEL CAJZL	PAVEL KRATKY
MARC CASS	DEREK LEA
STEVE CASWELL	DIMO LIPITKOVSKI
VIKTOR CERVENKA	GUY LIST
STUART CLARK	DAVID LISTVAN
ARIS COMNINOS	TONY LUCKEN
LAURIE CRANE	SEAN McCABE
RAY DE-HAAN	PETER MILES
JIM DOWDALL	JAN HOLICEK
NEIL FINNIGHAN	RAY NICHOLAS
STEVE GRIFFIN	DONAL O'FARRELL
PAUL HEASMAN	JAROSLAV PETERKA
LYNDON STUART HELLEWELL	
GARY POWELL	MARK HENSON
JAROSLAV PSENICKA	PAUL HERBERT
SEON ROGERS	DOMINIC HEWITT
MAC STEINMEIER	JEFF HEWITT-DAVIS
LEOS STRANSKY	JAN HOLICEK
TOM STRUTHERS	MARTIN HUB
PAVEL VOKOUN	DUSAN HYSKA
SHAUN WALLACE	ROB INCH
BILL WESTON	TIDDLER JAMES
MARK HANNA	RAY HANNA

THE CREW

Art Directors	RICKY EYRES
	TOM BROWN
	CHRIS SEAGERS
	ALAN TOMKINS
Standby Art Director	GARY FREEMAN
Assistant Art Director	KEVIN M. KAVANAUGH
Camera Operators	MITCH DUBIN
	CHRIS HAARHOFF
	SEAMUS CORCORAN
First Assistant Camera	STEVEN MEIZLER
	KENNY GROOM
	MARK MILSOME
Second Assistant Camera	TOM JORDAN
	ROBERT PALMER
Clapper/Loader	ROSALYN ELLIS
Camera Trainees	ALAN HALL
	ANGUS MITCHELL
Still Photographer	DAVID JAMES
Sound Mixer	RONALD JUDKINS
Boom Operator	ROBERT JACKSON
Cable Operator	DAVID MOTTA
First Assistant Editors	PATRICK CRANE
	RICHARD BYARD
Assistant Editors	MICHAEL TRENT
	ALEX GARCIA
	SIMON COZENS
	BRADLEY SOUBER
Apprentice Editor	JULIE ZUNDER

Supervising Sound Editor	RICHARD HYMNS
Re-Recording Mixers	GARY RYDSTROM
	GARY SUMMERS
	ANDY NELSON
Video Assist Operator	NOEL DONELLON
Video Assistant	SARAH FRANCIS
Script Supervisor	ANA MARIA QUINTANA
Chief Lighting Technician	DAVID DEVLIN
Rigging Chief Lighting Technician	OSSA MILLS
Best Boys	RICKY PATTENDEN
	RICHARD SEAL

Electricians

MAREK BOJSZA	NEIL MONROE
ALAN GROSCH	PETER O'TOOLE
DARREN GROSCH	STEVE PATTENDEN
PAUL KEMP	TERRY TOWNSEND

Key Grips	JAMES KWIATKOWSKI
	JOHN FLEMMING
Best Boy Grip	DEREK RUSSELL
Crane Grip	IAN TOWNSEND
"B" Camera Dolly Grip	DAVID RIST
Armourer	SIMON ATHERTON
Assistant Armourers	DEREK ATHERTON
	TOMMY DUNNE
	KARL SCHMIDT
Property Master	MAXIE McDONALD
Supervising Standby Props	MICKEY PUGH
Standby Props	MICKY WOOLFSON
Chargehand Props	STEPHEN McDONALD
Chargehand Dressing Props	JOHN HOGAN
Property Storage	ROBERT HILL

Props

JOHN FOX	DAVID ROSSITER
BARRY GATES	CHRISTIAN SHORT
CHRISTIAN McDONALD	BEN WILKINSON
PHILIP MURPHY	

Webbing Supervisor	ANDREW FLETCHER
Webbing Props	STEPHEN BROWN
	ALAN HAUSMANN
Production Buyer	DAVID LUSBY
Assistant Set Dressers	VERONIQUE FLETCHER
	PHILIPPA McLELLAN
Model Maker	KEITH STEPHEN
Illustrators	MATT CODD
	TIM FLATTERY
Art Department Coordinator	LAVINIA GLYNN-JONES
Art Department Assistants	JOANNA BRANCH
	PETER JAMES
	ERIC STEWART
Graphic Artist	LAWRENCE O'TOOLE
Draughtsmen	STEPHEN BREAM
	WILLIAM HAWKINS
	PAUL WESTACOTT
Jr. Draughtsmen	ROBERT COWPER
	MARGARET HORSPOOL
Special Effects Workshop Supervisor	TREVOR WOOD

Lead Sr. Special Effects Technicians

DAVID BRIGHTON	KEVIN HERD
PAUL CORBOULD	DAVE HUNTER
JOHN EVANS	

Sr. Special Effects Technicians

JEFF CLIFFORD	MARK MEDDINGS
IAN CORBOULD	MELVYN PEARSON
TERRY COX	PETER PICKERING
KENNETH HERD	PETER WHITE
RAY LOVELL	

Special Effects Technicians

MICHAEL BARLETT	JOHN PILGRIM
BRADLEY BARTON	GRAHAM POVEY
DANIEL BENNETT	SIMON QUINN
STEVE BORTHWICK	MELANIE RAYSKI

CAIMIN BOURNE — TONY RICHARDS
CHRISTOPHER BRENNAN — LEE RIDER
ALEX BURDETT — DAVE RODDHAM
PHILIP CLARK — GRANT ROGAN
SIMON COCKREN — KEVIN ROGAN
CLIFF CORBOULD — TIMOTHY STRACEY
MICHAEL CURRAN — PAUL TAYLOR
STUART DIGBY — COLIN UMPELBY
PAUL DIMMER — ANNE MARIE WALTERS
MICHAEL DURKAN — STEVEN WARNER
RAYMOND FERGUSON — DAVID WATKINS
JOHN FONTANA — DAVE WILLIAMS
JOSEPH GEDAY — TREVOR WILLIAMS
ADAM HILLIER — GARETH WINGROVE
ROB MALOS — ALAN YOUNG
DAVE MILLER

Special Effects Buyer — KRISSI WILLIAMSON
Special Effects Coordinator — CAROL McAULAY
Special Effects Assistant Buyer — KATIE GABRIEL
Prosthetics Supervisor — CONOR O'SULLIVAN
Prosthetics Designer — STUART SEWELL
Moldmaking Supervisor — JOHN SCHOONRAAD
Head Sculptor — ANDY HUNT
Prosthetic Crew
  MARTHA FEIN — ROBIN SCHOONRAAD
  EMMA JACKSON — TRISTAN SCHOONRAAD
  BRENDAN LONEGAN — LAURENCE SIMMONS
  DAN NIXON — KATRINA STRACHAN
  JACKIE NOBLE — GAVIN WATTON
Corpse and Animal
  Effects Designers — NEILL GORTON
    STEVE PAINTER
Corpse and Animal Effects
Coordinator — LINDY DIAMOND
Senior Sculptors
  STUART BRAY — DUNCAN JARMAN
  PAUL CATLING — WALDO MASON
  STUART CONRAN — PHILIP MATHEWS
  ANDY GARNER — COLIN WARE
Technicians
  CATH BLACKETT — WILL PETTY
  CHRIS BYRNE — ANDREW PROCTOR
  ARON COLLINS — LIZ RAGLAND
  LEE CRAIK — GRAHAM ROSS
  ANDREW FRANCE — PATRICK RUSHMERE
  JOANNE FRYE — JANINE SCHNEIDER
  BARRIE GOWER — ROBERT SIMPSON
  NINA GRAHAM — ROSIE SHANNON
  SAM IVES — ANNABEL TAIT
  VERONIQUE KEYS — BILL TURPIN
  ROB MAYOR — TANIA WANSTALL
  NICOLA O'TOOLE — SIMON WEBBER
  SUZI OWEN — JAMES WESTON
  ANTHONY PARKER — SHELLI WOODALL
Costume Supervisor — PAM WISE
Assistant Costume Designer — SALLY TURNER
Military Costumer — DAVID CROSSMAN
Costume Department Key — PATRICK WHEATLEY
Wardrobe Master — ANTHONY BLACK
Crowd Wardrobe Master — DAVE WHITEING
Key Set Costumer — TOM McDONALD
Set Costumers — MARCUS LOVE-McGUIRK
  ADAM ROACH
  LAURA MAY
Costumers — NIGEL BOYD
  RUPERT STEGGLE
  PETER EDMONDS
Key Costume Breakdown — TIMOTHY SHANAHAN
Costume Breakdown — THOMAS LIGHTFOOT
  EMMA WALKER
  NICOLA RAPLEY
Key Costume Special Effects/
  Stunts — PHILIP GOLDSWORTHY

Costume Special Effects/
  Stunts — PETER HORNBUCKLE
Workroom Head — DAVID EVANS
Seamstress — PAT WILLIAMSON
L.A. Key Costumer — DIANA WILSON
Costume Coordinator — SARAH HINCH
Costume Production Assistants — NATALIE ROGERS
  HELEN JEROME
Key Makeup Artist — LOIS BURWELL
Key Second Makeup Artist — PAULINE HEYS
Mr. Hanks' Makeup Artist — DANIEL C. STRIEPEKE
Makeup Artists — SIAN GRIGG
  CATHERINE HEYS
Trainee Makeup — POLLY EARNSHAW
Chief Hairstylist — JEANETTE FREEMAN
Hairstylist — TAPIO SALMI
Production Controller — JIM TURNER
Supervising Production Accountant — CAROLYN HALL
Production Accountant — GEORGE MARSHALL
Financial Representative — JAMES T. LINVILLE
Assistant Production Accountants — SOPHIE DASIC
  LISA-KIM LING KUAN
Accounting Assistants — CLAIRE KENNY
  ANDREW PYKE
  FRY MARTIN
Post Production Accountant — MARIA DeVANE
Production Coordinator — LIL HEYMAN
Assistant Production Coordinators — TANIA CLARKE
  LULU MORGAN
  RICK A. OSAKO
Second Second
Assistant Director — KAREN RICHARDS
Third Assistant Directors — MARTIN KRAUKA
  ANDREW WARD
Unit Publicist — SUE D'ARCY
Location Managers — ALEX GLADSTONE
  ROBIN HIGGS
Assistant Location Managers — SIMON BURGESS
  KATRYNA SAMUT-TAGLIAFERRO
  REBECCA JONES
  HUGO SMITH-BINGHAM
Assistants to Mr. Spielberg — KERI WILSON
  MARC FUSCO
Assistants to Mr. Spielberg – L.A. — SUSAN RAY
  ELIZABETH NYE
Assistant to Mr. Bryce — CARLYLE FAIRFAX SMITH
Assistant to Ms. Curtis — MARK RUSSELL
Assistant to Mr. Hanks — SHARON AIKEN
Production Associate — JASON ROBERTS
Production Assistants
  JANE BURGESS — GAIL MUNNELLY
  CARLOS FIDEL — AINE STACEY
Military Advisor — JOHN BARNETT
Casting Assistant – U.K. — ORLA PULTON
Casting Assistants – L.A. — KARA J. KATSULIS
  JEFF McNALLY
Construction Coordinator — TERRY APSEY
Assistant Construction Coordinator — JOHN NEW
Construction Buyer — HILLERY COPE
Supervising Carpenters — JOHN McGREGOR
  PAUL WILLIAMSON
  ANTHONY YOUD
Chargehand Carpenters — ALAN BOOTH
  FRED MYATT
  PHILLIP SMITH
Wood Machinists — NORMAN BAKER
  WILLIAM SOWER
Storesman — LOUIS KING
H.O.D. Plasterer — ALLAN CROUCHER
Supervising Plasterers — PETER BLACK
  MALCOLM MISTER
Chargehand Plasterer — KEITH SHANNON
Chargehand Plasterer Labourer — DAVID SILVERTON

H.O.D. Painter — ADRIAN START
Supervisor Painter — BRIAN MORRIS
H.O.D. Stagehand — KENNETH STACHINI
Chargehand/Stagehand — NIGEL ROSS
H.O.D. Rigger — RON NEWVELL
Supervisor Rigger — STEVEN POLLECUTT
Chargehand Rigger — JOHN NEWVELL
Welder — CHRISTOPHER ROSE
Welder Fabricator — COLIN GIBBS
Assistant Welder — MARK McBARRON
Plant Engineers — PAUL MALING
  STEVE TAYLOR
Standby Rigger — GINGER MacARTHY
Standby Carpenter — MICKY LAW
Standby Painter — JOE MONKS
Standby Plasterer — DEREK SMITH
Standby Stagehand — GERRY DELANEY
Transportation Coordinator — BRIAN HATHAWAY
Transportation Captain — BRIAN BAVERSTOCK
Mr. Spielberg's Driver — JOHN COLEMAN
Mr. Hanks' Driver — DAVID ROSENBAUM
Mr. Bryce's Driver — MIKE FAULKNER
Unit Drivers
  GARY BIRMINGHAM — BRUCE NEIGHBOUR
  FREDDIE CHIVERTON — SEAN O'CONNOR
  KEITH HORSLEY — BILLY TURNER
  BARRY LEONTI
Picture Vehicles by — PLUS FILM SERVICES
Picture Vehicle Coordinator — STEVE LAMONBY
Mechanics
  DAVE FORSTER — MICHAEL TOMBS
  ANDY GRAY — PETER TOMBS
  JOHN LEHEN — JOHN SYMONDSEN
Catering Services Provided by — SET MEALS
Catering Manager — DAVID REYNOLDS
Manager — SARA CHAPPELL
Head Chefs — COLIN ANDERSON
  SINJUN SMITH
Chef — ED ANDERSON
Assistant Chefs — SARAH LINTON
  BECKY WISEMAN
Nurse — CARRIE JOHNSON
Fire Safety Officer — DAVID DEANE
Firemen — CHRISTOPHER CULLUM
  BOB POLLARD

IRISH UNIT

Production Manager — SEAMUS McINERNEY
Camera Operator — CIAN DE BUTLEAR
First Assistant Camera — CIARAN BARRY
  DONAL GILLIGAN
Second Assistant Camera — DECLAN KING
  DOCHY J. LOWE
Chief Lighting Technician — TERRY MULLIGAN
Grip — PHILIP MURPHY
Electricians — GARRET BALDWIN
  PETER O'TOOLE
Props — WILLIAM DRAPER
  GARY WIFFEN
  COS EGAN
Senior Special Effects
  Technician — GERRY JOHNSTON
Special Effects Technicians — MICHAEL KEARNS
  KEVIN NOLAN
  ANDREW NOLAN
Marine Coordinator — ROBIN DAVIES
Marine Safety — ALISTER RUMBALL
Marine Riggers — DAN BRITTON
  ROGER McGOWAN
Shipwright — PAUL TINGEY
Marine Engineers — DAVE LESHONE
  GEOFF RALEIGH
Landing Craft Coordinator — KEN MURGATROYD

Landing Craft Crew
ALAN ARMSBY JOHN MURPHY
RUPERT BARNES NOEL MURPHY
COLIN BATES DAVID NEED
ROBERT BRIAN MICHAEL O'LEARY
STEPHEN DAWSON STEVE RICHARDS
PATRICK DEVEREUX GARY ROWE
ROBERT FOLEY MICK SELLEN
DONALD HIND STEVE SWEET
JOHN GEAR MICK THOMAS
DAVID KELLY RAY TOVEY
JAMES KINSELLA GERALD WADE
RONNIE LONGRIDGE BRIAN WALKER
DAVID McDOWALL SEAMUS WALSH
JASON MOONEY STUART WESTON
LINDSAY MOORE DAVID WINN
PETER MOORE
Costume Supervisor SHEILA FAHEY
Costume Assistants
FIONA BELTON OONA McFARLAND
MAEVE HUNTER ANN O'HALLORAN
COLETTE JACKSON ANN REGAN
LOUISE KEATING
Makeup Artists JENNIFER HEGARTY
AILBHE LE MASS
Hairstylist MARTINA McCARTHY
Assistant Hairstylist HUGH McALLISTER
Second Assistant Director CATHERINE DUNNE
Third Assistant Directors DAISY CUMMINS
BARBARA MULCAHY
HANNAH QUINN
Location Manager MELANIE GORE GRIMES
Assistant Location Managers JAMES CLONEY
DAVID MORRIS
Production Accountant DAVID MURPHY
Assistant Production
Accountants ANN-MARIE FITZGERALD
SIOBHAN SWEENEY
Production Coordinator ELAINE BURT
Asst. Production Coordinator CLODAGH BOWERS
Sign Writer LAURENCE O'TOOLE
Construction Managers MICHAEL DEEGAN
DAVID LOWERY
Production Office Assistants
MAEVE BUTLER DICKON LEVINGE
AILEEN CURTIN KATHLEEN LUCKING
LISA DRAYNE
Nurse SIOBHAN GRANT
Post Production Executive MARTIN COHEN
Post Production Supervisor ERICA FRAUMAN
Post Production Coordinator SVEN E. FAHLGREN
Post Production Sound
Services Provided by SKYWALKER SOUND
a division of Lucas Digital Limited, Marin County, CA
Effects Editors
ETHAN VAN DER RYN TERESA ECKTON
FRANK EULNER KAREN WILSON
LARRY OATFIELD
Dialogue Editors GWENDOLYN YATES WHITTLE
SARA BOLDER
EWA SZTOMPKE OATFIELD
Foley Editors SANDINA BAILO LAPE
BRUCE LACEY
Assistant Sound Designer SHANNON MILLS
Supervising Sound Assistants LISA CHINO
ANDRÉ FENLEY
Assistant Effects Editors DAN ENGSTROM
LARRY HOKI
Assistant Dialogue Editor MARY WORKS
Assistant Foley Editor SUSAN POPOVIC
Sound Intern GERARD ROCHE
Machine Room Supervisor RONALD G. ROUMAS
Mix Technician TONY SERENO

Machine Room Operator CHRISTOPHER BARRICK
Sound Transfer Supervisor MARNI L. HAMMETT
Digital Transfer JONATHAN GREBER
DEE SELBY
Video Services CHRISTIAN VON BURKLEO
JOHN TORRIJOS
ADR Supervisor LARRY SINGER
ADR Editors DENISE WHITING
THOMAS WHITING
ADR Assistant STEPHANIE D. KRIVACEK
ADR Mixer DEAN DRABIN
ADR Recordist CARY STRATTON
Foley Artists DENNIE THORPE
JANA VANCE
Foley Mixer TONY ECKERT
Foley Recordist FRANK MEREL
Re-Recordists RUDI PI
MATT COLLERAN
Engineer TOM LALLEY
ADR Group Coordinator MICKIE McGOWAN
Additional Re-Recording Services TODD-AO
STUDIOS WEST
Music Editor KEN WANNBERG
Assistant Music Editor KELLY MAHAN JARAMILLO
Post Production Associate MIKE CUEVAS
Orchestrations JOHN NEUFELD
*Score performed by members of the Boston Symphony
Orchestra and by the Tanglewood Festival Chorus*
Orchestral Personnel Manager LYNN G. LARSEN
Horn Solos GUS SEBRING
Trumpet Solos TIM MORRISON THOMAS ROLFS
Recorded and Mixed by SHAWN MURPHY
Score Recorded at SYMPHONY HALL, BOSTON
Scoring Consultant SANDY DeCRESCENT
Music Preparation JO ANN KANE MUSIC SERVICE
Executive in Charge of Music TODD HOMME
Special Visual
Effects by INDUSTRIAL LIGHT & MAGIC
A division of Lucas Digital Limited, Marin County, CA
Visual Effects Supervisor STEFEN FANGMEIER
Visual Effects Co-Supervisor ROGER GUYETT
Visual Effects Producer KIM BROMLEY
Associate Visual Effects Producer HEATHER SMITH
Visual Effects Art Director ALEXANDER LAURANT
Color Timing Supervisor KENNETH SMITH
CG Sequence Supervisor GREGOR LAKNER
Sabre Supervisor PABLO HELMAN
CG Artists
KATHLEEN BEELER TERRY CHOSTNER
GONZALO ESCUDERO BRIDGET GOODMAN
JOANNE HAFNER MARY McCULLOCH
JENNIFER McKNEW CHRISTA STARR
PAUL THEREN
Sabre Artists CAITLIN CONTENT
CHAD TAYLOR
Digital Matte Artist MATTHEW HENDERSHOT
Visual Effects Production Coordinator LORI ARNOLD
Visual Effects Editor BILL KIMBERLIN
Scanning Supervisor JOSHUA PINES
Visual Effects Camera
Operator MARTIN ROSENBERG
Visual Effects Camera Assistant ROBERT HILL
Lead Effects Technician GEOFF HERON
Effects Technician DAN NELSON
Stage Technicians CARL ASSMUS
BERNY DEMOLSKI
ROBERT DOHERTY
Film Scanning Operator GEORGE GAMBETTA
Negative Line-up TIM GEIDEMAN
Plate Restoration TRANG BACH
Digital Production
KATHLEEN DAVIDSON JENNIFER GONZALEZ
GARRICK MEEKER ERIN WEST

Digital Technologies DANNY LEE
JEFFREY YOST
Visual Effects Production
Assistant AMANDA MONTGOMERY
Color Timer DALE GRAHN
Negative Cutter GARY BURRITT
Titles & Opticals PACIFIC TITLE/MIRAGE

SONGS
"Solitude" Written by Duke Ellington, Irving Mills &
Eddie DeLange

"Tu Es Partout" Written by Edith Piaf &
Marguerite Monnot
"C'était Une Histoire
D'Amour" Written by Henri Contet & Jean Jal
Performed by Edith Piaf
Courtesy of Mercury Records, France
By arrangement with PolyGram Film & TV Music

Soundtrack Available on
DREAMWORKS RECORDS

Produced with the support of investment incentives
for the Irish film industry provided by the
government of Ireland.

THE PRODUCERS WISH TO THANK
THE FOLLOWING:
The British Film Commission
Welwyn Hatfield District Council
St. Albans District Council
The Residents of Welwyn & Hatfield
Herts Film Link
Arlington Property Developments
Irish Department of Arts, Culture and the Gaeltacht
Irish Department of Defense and Defense Forces
Irish Department of the Marine
The Cloney Family
Wexford County Council
The Residents of the City and
County of Wexford, Ireland
St. Peters College, Wexford
The U.S. Department of Defense
The American Battle Monuments Commission
20-20 Extras Casting
Fruit of the Loom
Range Rover
Mar-Key Marquees
Lee Lighting

Filmed on location in England, Ireland and France

Edited on the Moviola™

ACKNOWLEDGEMENTS
The publisher and editors wish to thank the
following for their special contributions to this book:
Stephen E. Ambrose, Sharon Black, Sheila Clarke,
Bonnie Curtis, Laura Fox, Brad Globe, Tom Hanks,
David James, Suzanne Jurva, Jane LeGate, Marvin Levy,
Anne McGrath, Randy Nellis, Boyd Peterson,
Terry Press, Robert Rodat, Mark Russell,
Heidi Schaeffer, Jerry Schmitz, Steven Spielberg,
Michael Vollman, Hurley West,
and Stephanie Wheeler.